The Basics Of Feng Shui: A Beginner's Guide

Margot Read

Published by Nimzo Media, 2024.

While every precaution has been taken in the preparation of this book, the publisher assumes no responsibility for errors or omissions, or for damages resulting from the use of the information contained herein.

THE BASICS OF FENG SHUI: A BEGINNER'S GUIDE

First edition. February 19, 2024.

ISBN: 979-8224978670

Written by Margot Read.

The Basics of Feng Shui: A Beginner's Guide

Table of Contents

11 Chapter 11: Feng Shui for Health and Well-being

12 Chapter 12: Feng Shui for Love and Relationships

13 Chapter 13: Feng Shui for Children's Spaces

14 Chapter 14: Feng Shui for Gardens and Outdoor Spaces

15 Chapter 15: Feng Shui for Personal Success and Growth

1 Cultivating Personal Development with Feng Shui
2 Enhancing Personal Achievement Areas
3 Creating Positive Energy for Personal Growth

Chapter 1: Introduction to Feng Shui

What is Feng Shui?

Have you ever walked into a room and instantly felt a sense of calm and serenity? Or perhaps you've entered a space that felt chaotic and overwhelming. All of these experiences can be attributed to the energy present in the environment.

Feng Shui teaches us that everything is connected and that the energy, or qi, within a space, can greatly impact our lives. Understanding and harnessing the energy flow can create a harmonious and balanced environment that supports our goals and aspirations.

So, how does energy flow within a space? Imagine a river flowing through the landscape. Just as the river meanders around obstacles and flows freely, energy moves through our spaces in a similar way. However, it can become blocked or stagnant if we don't pay attention to its flow.

One of the fundamental principles of Feng Shui is creating a clear and unobstructed path for energy to flow. This involves decluttering our spaces, organizing our belongings, and arranging furniture in a way that allows energy to move freely.

But it's not just about physical objects. The placement of doors, windows, and mirrors also plays a significant role in guiding energy throughout a space. By strategically positioning these elements, we can enhance energy flow and create a more positive and supportive environment.

Another important aspect of energy balance in Feng Shui is the concept of yin and yang. Yin represents the passive and receptive energy, while yang represents the active and dynamic energy. Balancing these two energies is crucial to creating a harmonious space.

When designing a room, it's important to consider the yin and yang qualities of each element. For example, soft and plush furniture can add a yin quality to a room, while bold and vibrant colors can create a yang energy. By finding the right balance between these contrasting energies, we can create a space that feels both relaxing and energizing.

By now, you may be realizing the incredible potential of Feng Shui in transforming your living or work environment. The principles of energy flow and balance are at the core of this ancient practice, and understanding them will empower you to create spaces that support your well-being and success.

History of Feng Shui

Now that we understand the basics of Feng Shui, let's delve into its fascinating history. By examining the origins and development of Feng Shui, we can gain a deeper understanding of how this ancient practice has shaped the world around us today.

Feng Shui, which translates to wind and water in English, traces its roots back thousands of years to ancient China. It emerged as a system for harmonizing individuals with their environment, with the belief that the arrangement of spaces and objects can influence their energy and well-being.

The origins of Feng Shui can be traced to the observations of early Chinese astronomers and farmers, who noticed a correlation between the orientation of their dwellings and the natural elements. They discovered that certain alignments and placements could create more favorable conditions, such as improved health, wealth, and relationships.

Over time, Feng Shui evolved and became intertwined with Chinese philosophy and beliefs. The principles of Yin and Yang, the Five Elements, and the I Ching (Book of Changes) played significant roles in shaping the practice. These ancient concepts provided a framework for understanding the balance and harmony between individuals and their surroundings.

Throughout history, Feng Shui was used not only for individual homes but also for important structures like palaces, temples, and tombs. It was believed that by applying Feng Shui principles, one could promote good fortune, prosperity, and even ward off negative energy or spirits.

As Chinese culture spread across Asia, Feng Shui gained popularity in neighboring countries such as Japan, Korea, and Vietnam. Its practical applications and spiritual significance resonated with people from all walks of life, regardless of their cultural or religious backgrounds.

Today, Feng Shui continues to be practiced and appreciated by people worldwide. Its principles have been adapted to modern living and integrated into contemporary architecture and interior design. Many individuals seek the guidance of Feng Shui experts to optimize their homes and workspaces, hoping to enhance not only their physical environment but also their overall well-being and success.

Understanding the origins and development of Feng Shui provides us with a deeper appreciation for the wisdom and timelessness of this ancient practice. By incorporating its principles into our lives, we can align ourselves with the natural flow of energy and create spaces that nurture our souls.

Benefits of Practicing Feng Shui

As we delve deeper into the fascinating world of Feng Shui, we begin to uncover the numerous positive impacts it can have on our overall well-being. The ancient practice of Feng Shui has been around for thousands of years and is based on the belief that our physical surroundings have a direct influence on our energy and life experiences. In this subchapter, we will explore the various benefits of practicing Feng Shui and how it can enhance different aspects of your life.

One of the key benefits of incorporating Feng Shui into your life is the ability to create a harmonious and balanced environment. By arranging your living or working space in accordance with Feng Shui principles, you can create a harmonious flow of energy that promotes a sense of peace and well-being. This can help to reduce stress, improve focus, and enhance overall productivity.

Another benefit of practicing Feng Shui is its ability to improve your relationships. Feng Shui teaches us that our physical environment can have a profound impact on our relationships with others. By creating a space that is welcoming and inviting, you can foster better communication, strengthen connections, and create a more harmonious atmosphere in your personal and professional relationships.

Feng Shui also has the potential to enhance your health and well-being. According to the principles of Feng Shui, the placement of objects and furniture in your space can affect your physical health. By optimizing the flow of Chi energy in your environment, you can support good health, promote relaxation, and create a space that is conducive to healing and rejuvenation.

Furthermore, practicing Feng Shui can bring about a greater sense of abundance and prosperity in your life. By aligning your space with the principles of Feng Shui, you can create an energetic environment that attracts positive energy and opportunities. This can lead to increased financial success, career growth, and overall abundance in your life.

Lastly, implementing Feng Shui principles can have a profound impact on your overall sense of well-being and happiness. By creating a space that is visually appealing, comfortable, and personalized, you can foster a sense of joy and contentment in your daily life. When you are surrounded by a supportive and nurturing environment, you are more likely to experience a greater sense of happiness and fulfillment.

As you can see, there are numerous benefits to practicing Feng Shui in your life. By understanding and applying the principles of Feng Shui, you can create a space that supports and enhances your well-being in various areas of your life. Whether it's improving your health, relationships, or overall happiness, Feng Shui has the potential to transform your life and help you thrive.

Chapter 2: The Five Elements of Feng Shui

Wood Element

In the previous chapter, we delved into the fascinating world of Feng Shui and explored the concept of the Wood element. Now, let's dive even deeper into understanding the characteristics and symbolism of the Wood element in Feng Shui.

The Wood element is associated with growth, vitality, and expansion. It represents new beginnings, creativity, and the energy of springtime. Just like the strong and sturdy trees in a forest, the Wood element in your space can bring a sense of balance, renewal, and vibrant energy.

When we embrace the Wood element, we invite the essence of nature into our surroundings. Imagine the fresh scent of a forest, the vibrant green leaves swaying in the breeze, and the gentle sound of birds chirping in the distance. Incorporating the Wood element into your space can create a similar ambiance, cultivating a harmonious and rejuvenating environment.

There are various ways to bring the Wood element into your space. Let's explore some ideas:

1. Introduce wooden furniture: Incorporate wooden furniture pieces, such as tables, chairs, or shelves, to bring the grounding and nurturing energy of the Wood element. Opt for sustainable and eco-friendly wood whenever possible.

2. Add plants and flowers: Plants and flowers are a wonderful way to infuse the Wood element into your space. Choose leafy green plants or arrange a bouquet of fresh flowers. Not only do they add beauty and color, but they also purify the air and create a connection with nature.

3. Use the color green: The color green is closely associated with the Wood element. Incorporate this soothing hue through paint, wall art, or decor items. It evokes feelings of renewal, growth, and tranquility.

4. Embrace natural textures: Incorporate natural textures, such as wooden flooring, burlap curtains, or rattan furniture, to enhance the Wood element's grounding and earthy energy. These textures add warmth and a sense of harmony to your space.

5. Display artwork inspired by nature: Hang artwork depicting landscapes, forests, or botanical motifs to celebrate the beauty and abundance of the Wood element. These pieces serve as a visual reminder of growth, vitality, and the interconnectedness of all living things.

Remember, the key is to find a balance and create a space that resonates with you. Experiment with different elements, textures, and colors until you achieve a harmonious atmosphere that promotes growth and vitality.

Now that you have a deeper understanding of the Wood element and how to incorporate it into your space, let's move on to the next chapter, where we'll explore more exciting ways to harness the power of Feng Shui.

Fire Element

As we continue our journey into the transformative powers of Feng Shui, we now delve deeper into the element of Fire. Fire is a symbol of passion, action, and transformation. When harnessed correctly, it can ignite the energy we need to create positive change in our lives.

Fire represents the dynamic and active qualities that we possess within ourselves. It is associated with the south direction and the summer season. Just like a flickering flame, Fire can illuminate our path and provide warmth and comfort. It is an essential element in Feng Shui as it provides the necessary energy and motivation to pursue our dreams and goals.

In Feng Shui, Fire is represented by colors such as red, orange, and yellow. These warm hues can bring vitality, enthusiasm, and creativity into our living spaces. Light and illumination are also important aspects of Fire, so be sure to incorporate lighting fixtures or candles to enhance the Fire energy in your home.

When working with the Fire element, it is essential to strike a balance. While Fire can bring passion and action, an excess of this energy can lead to impulsivity or aggression. Therefore, it is important to carefully integrate the Fire element in areas of your life and home where it can be appropriately channeled.

One way to bring the Fire element into your space is by focusing on the south area of your home or room. You can incorporate Fire-related decor or artwork, such as paintings with vibrant red colors or candle holders. Additionally, placing plants with red or orange flowers in this area can infuse it with the energy of Fire.

Another powerful way to harness the energy of Fire is through the use of the Bagua map. The south area of the Bagua represents fame and reputation, which are aspects closely associated with Fire. By enhancing this area with Fire-related elements, you can amplify the positive energy and attract recognition and success.

Remember, the key to effectively utilizing the Fire element is to be mindful of its energy and the intention behind its use. Fire can ignite passions, fuel actions, and inspire transformation, but it is up to us to harness its power in a balanced and constructive way.

As you explore the Fire element in Feng Shui, embrace the passion and motivation it brings. Let its vibrant energy guide you on a journey of personal growth, transformation, and fulfillment.

Earth Element

Welcome back! I hope you're enjoying your journey into the fascinating world of Feng Shui. In our previous chapter, we explored the concept of grounding and stabilizing qualities that the Earth element brings to your space. Now, let's delve deeper into the Earth element and discover how it can create a sense of balance and nourishment in your environment.

The Earth element in Feng Shui represents stability, nourishment, and grounding. It provides a solid foundation and a sense of security in your home or office. Just like the Earth itself, this element offers grounding energy that can help you feel more centered, stable, and connected to the present moment.

Earth energy is associated with qualities such as reliability, practicality, and patience. When this element is well-balanced and harmonious in your space, it can bring a sense of abundance, nurturing, and harmony into your life.

Imagine the feeling of walking barefoot on soft, fertile soil – that's the essence of the Earth element. It brings a soothing and comforting energy that helps us feel grounded, secure, and supported. By incorporating the Earth element into your space, you can create a peaceful sanctuary where you can recharge and find stability amidst the hustle and bustle of daily life.

Now that we understand the significance of the Earth element, let's explore how to incorporate it into your space to create an environment that is balanced and nourishing.

One way to bring the Earth element into your space is through color. Earthy tones such as beige, sandy browns, and soft yellows can evoke a sense of stability and groundedness. Consider using these colors in your furniture, decor, or even wall paint to infuse your space with Earth energy.

Another way to invite the Earth element is through texture. Choose materials such as stone, clay, or natural fibers like cotton and linen. These textures not only add a tactile richness to your space but also reinforce the Earth's grounding qualities.

Incorporating natural elements, like potted plants or crystals, can also enhance the Earth energy in your environment. Plants not only purify the air but also symbolize growth and abundance. Crystals, such as jasper or hematite, can provide a stabilizing influence and promote a sense of grounding.

Finally, cultivating a clutter-free space is essential in creating a balanced and grounded environment. Decluttering your space not only creates a sense of physical and mental organization but also allows the Earth energy to flow freely.

By incorporating the Earth element into your space, you can create a harmonious and balanced environment that supports your well-being and nourishes your soul. Embrace the grounding qualities that the Earth offers and watch as it brings stability and abundance into every aspect of your life.

Metal Element

Water Element

Welcome back! I'm excited to dive deeper into the fascinating world of Feng Shui with you. In the previous chapter, we explored the concept of energy flow and the different elements associated with it. Today, we will focus specifically on the Water element and how it can bring calm and clarity to your space.

The Water element in Feng Shui is known for its fluidity and adaptability. It symbolizes our emotions, intuition, and the flow of energy in our lives. Just like water can take on various forms, such as a serene lake or a powerful river, it has the ability to transform and adapt to its surroundings. Similarly, the Water element in your space can help you navigate through life's challenges and bring a sense of ease and tranquility.

Incorporating the Water element into your home or office can have a profound impact on your wellbeing. It can help create a sense of calm, promote clarity of thought, and even enhance your intuition. By harnessing the power of Water, you can create a space that supports your emotional well-being and allows you to connect with your inner self.

There are various ways to bring the Water element into your space. One simple method is by incorporating the color blue. Paint a wall in a soothing shade of blue or add blue accents through decorative items. Blue is often associated with tranquility and can instantly create a calming effect in a room.

Another way to harness the power of Water is by incorporating actual water features. A small tabletop fountain or a fish tank can introduce the element into your space and create a soothing ambiance. The sound of flowing water can be incredibly relaxing and can promote a sense of peace and serenity.

Additionally, you can bring the Water element into your space by using reflective surfaces. Mirrors, for example, can mimic the effects of water by reflecting light and creating a sense of depth. They also symbolize the ability to see beyond the surface and tap into your intuition.

Another key aspect of incorporating the Water element is through the use of symbols and imagery. Items such as seashells, images of oceans or rivers, or even artwork depicting water scenes can infuse your space with the qualities of Water. These symbols act as reminders of the element and can help evoke a sense of calm and clarity.

As you embark on your journey to create a harmonious and balanced environment, remember that the Water element can be a powerful tool in promoting a sense of calm and clarity. By incorporating the fluidity and adaptability of Water into your space, you can create an atmosphere that supports your emotional well-being and fosters a deeper connection with yourself.

Chapter 3: Applying Bagua in Feng Shui

Understanding Bagua

Welcome back! Now that you have a basic understanding of Feng Shui, let's dive deeper into one of its fundamental concepts: Bagua. Bagua is an essential tool in Feng Shui that helps us analyze and balance the energy in different areas of our space. It provides a map that represents different aspects of our lives and how they relate to specific areas within our home or office.

When we understand Bagua and how to use it effectively, we can make intentional choices about the placement of objects, furniture, and decor in our space to enhance the flow of energy and create harmony and balance in our lives.

So, what exactly is Bagua? Bagua is a grid-like map consisting of eight trigrams, each representing different aspects of our lives, such as wealth, health, relationships, career, and more. It is shaped like an octagon, with each of the eight trigrams placed in specific areas according to their corresponding life sector.

The purpose of using the Bagua map is to analyze the energy flow within our space and identify areas that may need attention or adjustments. By doing so, we can make changes that enhance the positive energy and minimize any negative influences that may be affecting different aspects of our lives.

To use the Bagua map effectively, we first need to understand how the eight trigrams correspond to different areas of our space. Each area represents a specific aspect of our lives, and by mapping them out, we can identify which areas need more focus and which areas are already in balance.

For example, the northern area of the Bagua map represents our career and life path. If this area of our space is cluttered or lacks any supportive elements, it may hinder our professional growth. On the other hand, if we have a clear and well-organized northern area, it can promote positive energy flow and help us thrive in our careers.

Similarly, other areas of the Bagua map correspond to different aspects of our lives such as health, relationships, creativity, and more. By analyzing these areas and making intentional adjustments, we can create a space that supports our goals and aspirations.

As you continue your journey into Feng Shui, learning about Bagua and how to incorporate it into your space will greatly enhance your ability to create harmony and balance. By understanding the relationship between your surroundings and different aspects of your life, you can make intentional choices that align with your goals and aspirations.

So, let's dive into the next chapter where we will explore the various aspects of the Bagua map in detail and learn how to use it to analyze and balance the energy in different areas of your space. Get ready to unlock the true potential of Feng Shui!

Bagua Areas and Their Associations

Now that we have a basic understanding of Feng Shui and its principles, let's dive deeper into the Bagua areas and their corresponding associations. The Bagua is an essential tool in Feng Shui, as it helps us map out the different areas of our home or space and their connection to specific aspects of our life.

There are eight Bagua areas, each representing a different aspect of our life. By understanding these areas and their associations, we can make targeted enhancements and adjustments to create a more harmonious and balanced environment that supports our goals and aspirations.

1. Career: The Career area is connected to our professional life, success, and opportunities for growth. By enhancing this area, we can attract new career opportunities, improve our job prospects, and increase our chances of advancement.

2. Knowledge: The Knowledge area is associated with self-improvement, education, and personal growth. By focusing on this

area, we can enhance our learning abilities, expand our knowledge, and open doors to new opportunities for personal and intellectual development.

3. Family: The Family area relates to our relationships with our family members and the harmony within our household. By enhancing this area, we can promote greater understanding, love, and support among family members, creating a nurturing and harmonious home environment.

4. Wealth: The Wealth area is connected to abundance, prosperity, and financial well-being. By activating this area, we can attract opportunities for wealth creation, increase our income, and improve our overall financial situation.

5. Fame: The Fame area is associated with our reputation, recognition, and public image. By energizing this area, we can enhance our personal charisma, gain the respect and admiration of others, and boost our chances of success in our chosen field.

6. Relationships: The Relationships area focuses on our romantic relationships, partnerships, and social connections. By harmonizing this area, we can attract loving and supportive relationships, improve existing partnerships, and cultivate a sense of balance and fulfillment in our personal connections.

7. Creativity: The Creativity area is connected to artistic expression, innovation, and creative endeavors. By activating this area, we can tap into our creative potential, enhance our problem-solving abilities, and infuse our life with inspiration and imagination.

8. Health: The Health area relates to our physical well-being and overall vitality. By energizing this area, we can promote good health, increase energy levels, and create a nurturing environment that supports our well-being.

Each of these Bagua areas has specific associations and enhancements that can be applied to create a harmonious and balanced space. In the next section, we will explore these associations and learn how to apply them to our own homes or spaces.

Ways to Use Bagua in Your Space

Now that you've learned the basics of Feng Shui and the principles of Bagua, it's time to dive into the practical tips and techniques for applying these principles in your space. In this section, I'll share with you some ways to use Bagua in your home or office that will help you align your space with your goals and intentions.

1. Rearrange your furniture: One of the most effective ways to incorporate Bagua in your space is to rearrange your furniture in accordance with the Bagua map. By aligning your furniture with each area of the map, you can create a harmonious flow of energy and enhance different aspects of your life. For example, placing your desk in the Knowledge and Wisdom area can promote focus and learning, while positioning your bed in the Relationship area can improve your romantic relationships.

2. Use colors strategically: Colors have a powerful impact on our emotions and energy levels. By using colors strategically in each area of the Bagua map, you can enhance the desired energy of that space. For instance, using shades of green and brown in the Family and Health area can promote a sense of grounding and vitality, while incorporating shades of red or pink in the Love and Relationship area can stimulate passion and romance.

3. Declutter and organize: Clutter can disrupt the flow of energy in your space, so it's important to declutter and organize regularly. By clearing out physical clutter, you make room for fresh energy to circulate and rejuvenate your environment. Take the time to go through your belongings and let go of items that no longer serve you. This will create a harmonious and inviting atmosphere in your home or office.

4. Incorporate natural elements: Nature has a soothing and grounding effect on us, so it's beneficial to incorporate natural elements

in your space. You can introduce plants to bring in the energy of growth and vitality, use natural materials like wood and stone for furniture and decor, and let in natural light as much as possible. Connecting with the elements of nature will help create a balanced and harmonious environment.

5. Personalize your space: Your space should reflect your personality and preferences. Add personal touches such as photographs, artwork, or sentimental objects that uplift your mood and inspire you. Surround yourself with things that bring you joy and make you feel connected to your space. When you feel a deep sense of comfort and belonging in your environment, it positively influences your overall well-being and productivity.

By implementing these practical tips and techniques, you'll be able to create a space that supports and nurtures you in achieving your goals. Remember, Bagua is not just about physical adjustments in your space; it's also about cultivating a mindset of intention and mindfulness.

Chapter 4: Yin and Yang in Feng Shui

Understanding Yin and Yang

Now that we have explored the fundamental concepts of Yin and Yang in Feng Shui, it's time to delve deeper into the understanding of these energies. In this subchapter, we will take a closer look at the concept of Yin and Yang and how they interact with each other.

Yin and Yang are two opposing forces that exist in everything in the universe. Yin represents the feminine energy, associated with darkness, passivity, and introspection. On the other hand, Yang represents the masculine energy, associated with light, activity, and extroversion. These energies are not independent of each other but rather interdependent and interconnected.

The concept of Yin and Yang is all about finding balance and harmony between these two energies. In Feng Shui, it is essential to understand the interplay between Yin and Yang and how to create a harmonious environment that promotes the flow of energy.

One way to understand Yin and Yang is through the concept of duality. Just as day cannot exist without night and there is no light without darkness, Yin and Yang complement each other. They are like two sides of the same coin, each containing a small amount of the other within itself.

Yin and Yang energies also manifest in different aspects of our lives. For example, the Yin energy is associated with softness, intuition, and receptivity, while the Yang energy is associated with strength, action, and assertiveness. Understanding these energies can help us make conscious decisions about our living spaces and create environments that support our goals and well-being.

When we embrace both Yin and Yang energies in our lives, we can achieve a sense of harmony and balance. By understanding the interplay between feminine and masculine energies, we can create spaces that promote relaxation, productivity, and overall well-being. Whether it's balancing the Yin and Yang energies in our homes or workplaces, Feng Shui provides us with the tools to create spaces that align with our intentions and aspirations.

Balancing Yin and Yang Energies

In this subchapter, we will delve into the fascinating concept of balancing Yin and Yang energies in your space. As we discovered in the previous chapter, finding harmony and balance between these two complementary forces is essential for creating a harmonious and energizing environment. Now, let's embark on a journey to explore how we can balance Yin and Yang energies in our space!

To create a balanced space, we must first identify and understand the Yin and Yang aspects present in our surroundings. Yin represents the passive, feminine, and cooling energy, while Yang symbolizes the active, masculine, and warming energy. By observing different elements and features in our space, we can determine if they predominantly embody Yin or Yang qualities.

Let's start by examining some common characteristics associated with Yin and Yang energies. Yin elements may include softer textures, cooler colors, gentle lighting, and rounded shapes. On the other hand, Yang elements often encompass brighter shades, sharper angles, stronger lighting, and more energetic patterns.

Once we have identified the Yin and Yang aspects in our space, we can then work towards achieving a harmonious balance between them. Balance is crucial because an excess of either Yin or Yang can disrupt the flow of energy and create disharmony.

One way to balance Yin and Yang energies is by introducing elements that embody the complementary force. For example, if your space feels overly Yin, you can incorporate some Yang qualities by adding vibrant colors, bold patterns, or sharper lines. Conversely, if your space feels excessively Yang, you can introduce Yin elements such as softer textures, muted tones, or soothing lighting.

Remember, achieving balance is not about eliminating one energy in favor of the other but rather finding a harmonious blend that supports optimal energy flow. By consciously creating a balance between Yin and Yang in your space, you can enhance the overall energy and promote a sense of harmony and well-being.

Now that we understand the importance of balancing Yin and Yang energies, let's move on to the practical techniques for addressing specific imbalances in our space. In the next section, we will explore how to identify and rectify Yin or Yang imbalances to ensure that our energy flow remains in optimal condition. Get ready to learn valuable insights and empowering strategies!

Incorporating Yin and Yang in Your Home

I'm thrilled to continue our exploration of incorporating Yin and Yang principles in your interior design. In this section, we will delve into creating a harmonious and balanced environment that supports your well-being.

Nowadays, people are becoming increasingly aware of the connection between the spaces they inhabit and their overall well-being. We all want our homes to be a sanctuary, a place where we can relax, rejuvenate, and find balance. By incorporating Yin and Yang principles, we can create a space that promotes harmony and enhances our physical and mental well-being.

So, let's dive straight into some practical ways to bring Yin and Yang into your home.

Chapter 5: The Role of Chi in Feng Shui

What is Chi?

So, what exactly is Chi? Understanding this concept is essential for anyone looking to explore the basics of Feng Shui. Chi is the vital life force energy that flows through everything in the universe, including our bodies, homes, and environments.

Imagine Chi as a river that constantly moves and circulates throughout our surroundings. Just like a river, Chi has different qualities and characteristics that can influence our well-being and overall energy levels.

One of the main goals of Feng Shui is to ensure that Chi flows harmoniously and freely in our living spaces, promoting positive energy and balance in our lives. By understanding and harnessing the power of Chi, we can create an environment that supports our goals and aspirations.

So, how can we tap into this mystical life force energy? Well, it all starts with a deep awareness of our surroundings and a willingness to make adjustments to enhance the flow of Chi.

Chi can be influenced by various factors such as the arrangement of furniture, the placement of objects, and the use of colors and materials in our spaces. By making intentional choices in these areas, we can invite positive Chi into our lives and promote a sense of harmony and balance.

But Chi isn't just limited to our physical environments. It also plays a significant role in our personal energy levels and overall well-being. By paying attention to our thoughts, emotions, and daily habits, we can cultivate a strong and vibrant Chi within ourselves.

So, my friend, let's embark on this journey together. Let's dive deeper into the world of Chi and explore its qualities and characteristics. By understanding the power of Chi, we can unlock the potential for positive change and transformation in our lives.

Enhancing Chi Flow in Your Environment

Now that you have learned the basics of Feng Shui and how it can positively impact your space, it's time to dive deeper into enhancing the flow of Chi in your environment. In this section, I will share with you some techniques and tips that will help you promote a smooth and balanced flow of energy in your space.

One of the key aspects of Feng Shui is enhancing the Chi flow in your environment. Chi, also known as life force energy, plays a vital role in our physical, mental, and emotional well-being. When the Chi energy in our surroundings is stagnant or imbalanced, it can affect various aspects of our lives.

To create a harmonious and energetically supportive space, it's important to focus on enhancing the flow of Chi. Here are some techniques that you can start implementing right away:

- Clear the clutter: Clutter can disrupt the flow of Chi energy in your space. Take the time to declutter and organize your environment, getting rid of anything that no longer serves a purpose or brings you joy.
- Air and light: Open windows and let fresh air circulate in your space. Natural light is also important for promoting a positive flow of energy. Make sure you have good ventilation and ample light sources in your home or office.
- Balance the elements: The five elements, namely wood, fire, earth, metal, and water, are essential in Feng Shui. Create a balanced representation of these elements in your space to enhance the flow of Chi. For example, you can incorporate plants for the wood element, candles for fire, and a small water feature for water.
- Remove obstacles: Take a look around your space and identify any physical obstacles that might be blocking the Chi flow. It could be furniture placed in a way that obstructs movement or cluttered pathways. Rearrange your furniture and create clear pathways to allow the Chi energy to flow freely.
- Use mirrors strategically: Mirrors are powerful tools in Feng Shui. They can be used to reflect and amplify Chi energy. Place mirrors in areas where you want to enhance the flow of Chi, such as near windows or in corners that need more light and energy.
- Introduce natural elements: Nature has a calming and revitalizing effect on our energy. Bring in natural elements like

plants, crystals, and natural materials to create a connection with the earth element and promote a balanced flow of Chi.

By implementing these techniques, you can create a space that supports the smooth and balanced flow of Chi energy. Remember, Feng Shui is a continuous practice, and it's important to regularly assess and adjust your space to maintain its energetic quality.

In the next section, we will explore how you can further enhance the energetic quality of your environment to support your overall well-being. Get ready to unleash the positive energy that Feng Shui can bring to your life!

Utilizing Feng Shui Cures for Chi

Now that we have a basic understanding of Feng Shui remedies and cures, it's time to delve deeper into the world of balancing energy in different areas of your home. In this section, I will guide you through the process of utilizing Feng Shui cures for Chi, helping you create a harmonious and balanced living space that promotes positive energy flow and overall well-being. So let's get started!

One popular Feng Shui cure for enhancing Chi is the use of mirrors. Mirrors have the power to reflect and redirect energy, making them a valuable tool in harmonizing your home. You can strategically place mirrors in areas where the energy feels stagnant or blocked. For example, if you notice a dark corner in a room where Chi seems to be inhibited, hang a mirror on the adjacent wall to help expand the space and allow energy to flow freely. Remember to avoid placing mirrors directly facing the main entrance or reflecting the bed, as this can disrupt the energy balance.

Another effective Feng Shui cure for promoting positive Chi is the use of plants. Plants not only add beauty and freshness to your home but also help to purify the air and promote a sense of tranquility. Incorporating plants with rounded leaves, such as the money plant or peace lily, can enhance the flow of Chi and create a more vibrant and harmonious environment. Be mindful of the placement of your plants - avoid placing them in the bedroom or in areas with excessive moisture, as this can negatively affect the energy balance.

Crystals and gemstones are also powerful Feng Shui cures that can be used to enhance Chi. Different crystals have different properties, so it's important to choose ones that align with your intentions. For example, amethyst promotes tranquility and spiritual growth, while citrine attracts abundance and prosperity. You can display crystals in different areas of your home or wear them as jewelry to benefit from their energy-enhancing properties. Just remember to cleanse and recharge your crystals regularly to maintain their effectiveness.

Lastly, incorporating the elements of nature can help to balance the energy in your home. The five elements - wood, fire, earth, metal, and water - each have their unique qualities and can be represented through colors, materials, and shapes. For example, to introduce the wood element, you can use green-colored objects or incorporate wooden furniture. Adding candles or a fireplace can represent fire, while earth can be represented through pottery or stone decor. By incorporating these elements thoughtfully, you can create a harmonious and balanced energy flow throughout your space.

Utilizing Feng Shui cures for Chi is an art that requires careful consideration and intention. By implementing these remedies into your home, you can tap into the positive energy flow and create an environment that supports your well-being and aspirations. Stay motivated and open-minded as you experiment with different cures and observe the positive changes that unfold. Remember, Feng Shui is a lifelong journey, and as you continue to deepen your understanding, you'll uncover even more ways to enhance the positive flow of Chi in your life.

Chapter 6: Feng Shui Tips for Entryways and Doors

The Importance of Entryways and Doors

The Importance of Entryways and Doors

Welcome back! Let's dive deeper into the fascinating world of Feng Shui and explore the significance of entryways and doors. You may not realize it, but the entryway to your home plays a crucial role in determining the energy flow and overall harmony within your living space. It sets the stage for the energy that enters your home and creates a first impression not only for your guests but also for the energy itself.

In Feng Shui, the main entrance is regarded as the mouth of your home, through which energy and opportunities enter. It serves as the gateway between the outside world and your private sanctuary. Imagine your home as a living organism, and the entryway as its mouth - it's where nourishment and vital energy are taken in. Just like you wouldn't want to consume unhealthy or negative substances, you want to ensure that the energy that enters your home is positive, vibrant, and life-enhancing.

Your entryway is also a reflection of your own energy and the energy you wish to invite into your life. By creating a welcoming and harmonious entrance, you are setting the stage for positive experiences and opportunities to flow into your life effortlessly. It's like rolling out a red carpet for abundance, success, and happiness.

So how can you optimize your entryway to harness its full potential? Here are a few simple yet powerful tips:

- Make sure your entryway is well-lit and free from clutter. Cleanliness and brightness attract positive energy and create a sense of expansiveness.
- Add plants and flowers to bring in nature's vitality and freshness. They help purify the energy and create a soothing,

welcoming atmosphere.

- Consider the color scheme of your entrance. Earthy tones like warm browns and subtle yellows promote a sense of grounding and stability, while vibrant colors like red or orange can bring in a lively and dynamic energy.

- Pay attention to the functionality and aesthetics of your front door. It should be in good condition, opening smoothly and easily. A welcoming entrance not only invites positive energy but also makes a lasting impression on visitors.

- You can also incorporate symbols of protection and good luck, such as a welcome mat with a meaningful message or a decorative charm to invite positive vibes into your home.

By investing a little time and effort into your entryway, you can create a powerful first impression and set the stage for positive energy to flow into your home. Remember, your front door acts as a gateway to the abundance of opportunities that await you. So why not make it a grand entrance? Embrace the power of Feng Shui and watch as your home becomes a magnet for positive energy, harmony, and prosperity.

Feng Shui Tips for Enhancing Entryways

I'm thrilled to continue our exploration of creating a welcoming and auspicious entryway. In this section, we'll dive into the fascinating world of Feng Shui and learn some valuable tips for enhancing our entryways. Let's get started!

Feng Shui, an ancient Chinese practice, enables us to harmonize the energy flow in our homes and create a positive and inviting atmosphere. By applying Feng Shui principles to our entryway, we can attract abundance, good fortune, and positive opportunities into our lives.

The first step in enhancing our entryway's Feng Shui is to ensure it is well-lit. Bright lighting not only uplifts the energy but also creates a warm and welcoming ambiance for anyone who visits. Consider installing a beautiful overhead light fixture or adding strategic lighting elements such as wall sconces or stylish table lamps.

Another essential Feng Shui tip is to keep your entryway clutter-free. A cluttered space can hinder the flow of positive energy and create a sense of stagnation. Take the time to declutter and remove any unnecessary items, allowing space for the energy to circulate freely. Place a tasteful storage solution near your entryway to keep essentials neatly organized.

Next, let's talk about the power of color. Choose a color scheme for your entryway that aligns with the energy you want to invite into your home. For example, vibrant red or orange hues symbolize good luck and happiness, while soothing blues and greens promote tranquility and abundance. Select a color palette that resonates with you and reflects the energy you wish to attract.

Incorporating natural elements into your entryway is another excellent way to enhance its Feng Shui. Place a few potted plants or fresh flowers near your front door to bring in the vibrant energy of nature. These living elements not only add beauty but also purify the air and lift the overall energy of the space.

Furthermore, consider using mirrors strategically in your entryway. Mirrors have the power to amplify positive energy and reflect it back into the space. Hang a mirror near your front door to create a sense of spaciousness and invite beneficial energy to flow.

Lastly, pay attention to the symbolism of your entryway. A plaque or artwork that represents good luck, prosperity, or harmony can infuse positive energy into the space. Choose pieces that resonate with you and evoke a sense of joy and positivity.

Remember, applying Feng Shui principles to your entryway is a fun and transformative process. By incorporating these tips, you'll create a beautiful and energetically vibrant space that attracts abundance and positive experiences into your life. Get ready for an amazing journey!

Creating a Welcoming and Harmonious Doorway

In the previous chapter, we discussed the importance of creating a harmonious and inviting entrance. Now, let's dive deeper into the topic and explore some design and decor strategies to help you achieve that. Get ready to transform your doorway into a warm and welcoming space!

When it comes to creating a welcoming and harmonious doorway, selecting the right color scheme can make a world of difference. Colors have the power to evoke certain emotions and set the mood of a space. For a front entrance, consider using warm and inviting colors such as earth tones, soft blues, or neutrals. These colors promote a sense of calmness and create a positive first impression for your guests.

Now, let's focus on lighting. Adequate lighting not only enhances the aesthetics of your doorway but also ensures safety and security. Consider installing a combination of ambient, task, and accent lighting. A well-placed and well-lit entrance creates a welcoming atmosphere for visitors, making them feel safe and invited.

Next, let's discuss the importance of incorporating natural elements into your doorway design. Nature has a soothing effect, so bringing in elements like plants, flowers, and natural materials can create a harmonious and inviting space. Consider placing potted plants near your front entrance or add a touch of greenery with a hanging basket. Furthermore, incorporating natural materials like wood or stone into your doorway design adds warmth and elegance to the space.

Now, let's move on to the importance of organization and decluttering. A cluttered entrance can create a sense of chaos and immediately put off guests. To create a harmonious and inviting entrance, ensure that your doorway is free of excessive clutter. Install hooks or a coat rack for guests to hang their coats or bags. Also, consider adding storage solutions like a shoe rack or a console table with drawers to keep things tidy and organized.

Lastly, don't forget about personalization! Adding personal touches to your front entrance can make it feel more welcoming and inviting.

Hang a personalized welcome sign or place a doormat with a warm greeting at your doorstep. You can also display some meaningful artwork or photographs in the entrance area to make it feel like home.

By implementing these design and decor strategies, you can create a harmonious and inviting entrance that will leave a positive first impression on your guests and visitors. Get creative, have fun, and enjoy transforming your doorway into a warm and welcoming space!

Chapter 7: Feng Shui in the Bedroom

Optimal Bedroom Layout and Design

Now that you have a good understanding of the basics of Feng Shui, it's time to dive into the exciting world of bedroom layout and design. Creating an ideal environment for rest and relaxation is essential for promoting a sense of peace and balance in your life. In this subchapter, we will explore the optimal layout and design principles for a Feng Shui bedroom, and how you can arrange your furniture and décor to promote restful sleep.

When it comes to creating a Feng Shui bedroom, it's important to consider the ideal layout and design principles that will enhance the flow of energy and promote a sense of calm and tranquility.

First, let's start with the bed. The bed should be placed in a commanding position, which means it should have a clear view of the door without being directly in line with it. This position allows you to feel safe and in control while you sleep. Make sure the headboard is against a solid wall for added stability and support.

Next, consider the placement of other furniture in the bedroom. Keep it to a minimum to maintain a spacious and open feel. Avoid placing furniture, such as desks or workout equipment, in the bedroom as they can create a sense of restlessness and disrupt the flow of energy. Instead, create a separate space in your home for work or exercise. This will allow your bedroom to be a sanctuary dedicated solely to rest and relaxation.

When it comes to colors and décor, choose soothing and calming shades such as soft blues, gentle greens, and neutral tones. Avoid bright and vibrant colors that can be overly stimulating and disrupt your sleep. Use natural materials like wood and cotton to create a harmonious and grounding atmosphere.

Consider incorporating elements of nature into your bedroom design. Hang artwork or photographs that depict peaceful landscapes or use plants to bring a sense of life and vitality. Keep the space clutter-free and organized to promote a clear and peaceful mind.

Remember, the ultimate goal of a Feng Shui bedroom is to create a space that promotes relaxation and restful sleep. By following these layout and design principles, you can create an environment that supports your well-being and helps you achieve a state of balance and harmony.

Harmonizing Relationships with Feng Shui in the Bedroom

When it comes to improving the quality of our relationships and enhancing intimacy, Feng Shui can play a significant role. By understanding the principles of Feng Shui and applying them to our living spaces, we can create a harmonious and nurturing environment for love and romance to flourish.

One of the key areas where we can implement Feng Shui strategies is in the bedroom. The bedroom is a sacred space where we seek rest, rejuvenation, and intimacy. By harmonizing this space with Feng Shui, we can create an environment that supports and enhances our relationships.

So how exactly can we harmonize our relationships with Feng Shui in the bedroom? Let's explore some practical tips and techniques:

1. Clear the clutter: Clutter in the bedroom can hinder the flow of energy and create a sense of chaos. Take the time to declutter your space, removing any items that are no longer serving a purpose or holding emotional baggage. By creating a clean and organized environment, you are allowing the energy to flow freely, creating a sense of calm and harmony.

2. Create a balanced layout: The layout of your bedroom plays a crucial role in creating a harmonious space. Position your bed in a commanding position, where you have a clear view of the entrance without being directly in line with it. This placement symbolizes stability, security, and control in your relationship. Avoid placing your bed under a window or directly in line with the door, as this can disrupt the flow of energy.

3. Choose soothing colors: The colors you choose for your bedroom can have a profound impact on your relationships. Opt for calming and soothing colors such as soft neutrals, pastels, or shades of blue and green. These colors promote relaxation and serenity, creating an atmosphere conducive to intimacy and deep connection.

4. Enhance the energy flow with plants: Adding living plants to your bedroom can help enhance the flow of positive energy and promote a sense of well-being. Choose plants with rounded leaves or flowers to create a gentle and nurturing energy. Avoid plants with pointed or sharp leaves, as they can create a more aggressive energy.

5. Create a romantic atmosphere: Lighting plays a crucial role in creating a romantic atmosphere in the bedroom. Replace harsh overhead lights with soft, warm lighting options such as table lamps or dimmer switches. Consider incorporating candles or Himalayan salt lamps for a soothing and intimate glow. Remember to keep the lighting balanced and symmetrical on both sides of the bed.

6. Personalize with meaningful items: Infuse your bedroom with personal touches that hold special meaning for you and your partner. Display cherished photographs, artwork, or sentimental objects that evoke positive emotions and memories. These meaningful items have the power to create a sense of connection and intimacy within the space.

By implementing these Feng Shui strategies in your bedroom, you can create a harmonious and nurturing space that supports and enhances your relationships. Take the time to assess your bedroom and make the necessary adjustments to align the energy in the space. Remember, creating a loving and intimate environment starts with creating a loving and intimate space.

Soothing and Relaxing Bedroom Colors

Now that we have delved into the fascinating world of color psychology and its impact on our emotional well-being, it's time to put our knowledge into action and explore the best colors and color combinations for creating a peaceful and serene bedroom environment.

When it comes to choosing soothing and relaxing colors for our bedroom, there are a few key factors to consider. First and foremost, we want colors that promote a sense of calm and tranquility, helping us unwind and prepare for a restful night's sleep.

One color that is often associated with relaxation is blue. Its cool tones evoke a sense of serenity and can help lower blood pressure and reduce stress levels. Light shades of blue, such as soft pastels or pale aqua, are particularly soothing and create a serene atmosphere in the bedroom.

Another color that promotes relaxation is green. The color of nature, green is known for its calming and rejuvenating properties. It brings a sense of harmony and balance to a space, making it ideal for creating a tranquil bedroom environment. Shades of sage, mint, or fern green can be particularly soothing and refreshing.

In addition to blue and green, neutral colors such as beige, taupe, and ivory can also create a peaceful ambiance in the bedroom. These soft understated hues provide a blank canvas for relaxation and allow other elements in the room to shine, such as natural textures and comforting textiles.

When it comes to choosing the best color combinations for a soothing bedroom, there are a few options to consider. One popular combination is blue and white. The crisp and clean look of white paired with the calming effect of blue creates a serene and airy atmosphere. This combination is perfect for those who prefer a minimalist and fresh bedroom aesthetic.

For a more earthy and organic feel, consider combining shades of green and brown. The natural tones of green and brown complement each other beautifully and evoke a sense of grounding and tranquility.

This combination is particularly suitable for those who appreciate a rustic or bohemian style in their bedroom.

Lastly, if you're looking for a sophisticated and luxurious bedroom environment, consider pairing neutral colors such as beige and gray. This combination exudes elegance and creates a serene and timeless space. Add touches of metallic accents or plush textures to elevate the overall aesthetic.

Remember, the key to creating a soothing and relaxing bedroom environment is to choose colors that resonate with you personally and promote a sense of calm. Experiment with different shades and combinations until you find the perfect palette that helps you unwind and recharge.

Next, we will explore the art of arranging furniture and decor in a way that enhances the peaceful and serene atmosphere of your bedroom. Let's dive in!

Chapter 8: Feng Shui in the Kitchen

Feng Shui Tips for Kitchen Organization

So, you're ready to dive into the world of Feng Shui and take your kitchen organization to the next level! In this section, I'll be sharing some practical tips that will help you declutter and organize your kitchen using the principles of Feng Shui. Get ready to create a clean and efficient kitchen space that supports the flow of positive energy.

1. Keep your countertops clear: One of the key principles of Feng Shui is promoting a sense of spaciousness and flow. To achieve this in your kitchen, it's important to keep your countertops clear of unnecessary clutter. Only have the essentials, such as a cutting board, knife block, and a few essential kitchen gadgets. By clearing your countertops, you'll create a more harmonious and inviting space.

2. Organize your cabinets and drawers: Take a moment to go through your kitchen cabinets and drawers. Remove any items that you no longer use or need. Group similar items together and keep them in designated areas. This will make it easier for you to find what you need and create a sense of order in your kitchen.

3. Establish a designated space for each item: In Feng Shui, everything has its place. Assign a specific spot for each item in your kitchen. This will not only help you stay organized but also promote a sense of harmony and balance. For example, keep your pots and pans in one area, your spices in another, and your utensils in a separate drawer.

4. Clear out expired and unused items: It's common for our kitchen cabinets and pantry to become a storage space for expired or unused items. Take the time to go through your food items and get rid of anything that is expired or no longer needed. By doing this, you'll create space for fresh and positive energy to flow into your kitchen.

5. Create a sense of symmetry: Another Feng Shui principle is creating a sense of balance and symmetry. In your kitchen, aim for symmetry in the placement of your appliances, utensils, and decorative elements. This will create a visually pleasing and harmonious space.

6. Use colors strategically: Colors can have a significant impact on the energy of a space. In your kitchen, consider using colors that promote a sense of nourishment and warmth. Earthy tones like beige, yellow, and green can create a soothing and inviting atmosphere. Avoid using dark or overpowering colors, as they can disrupt the flow of positive energy.

7. Enhance natural light and ventilation: Natural light and fresh air are essential elements in creating a positive and energetic kitchen space. Make sure to open up your windows whenever possible to let in natural light and fresh air. If your kitchen lacks natural light, consider using artificial lighting that mimics the qualities of daylight.

8. Incorporate plants and natural elements: Bringing nature into your kitchen can have a calming and refreshing effect. Consider adding potted plants or fresh flowers to your kitchen countertops or windowsills. Incorporate natural elements such as wooden cutting boards, bamboo utensils, or stone countertops to create a connection with the earth element.

By applying these practical Feng Shui tips, you'll be able to transform your kitchen into a space that is not only organized and efficient but also supports the flow of positive energy. Get ready to embrace the power of Feng Shui and create a kitchen that brings joy and nourishment to your life!

Enhancing Health and Abundance in the Kitchen

Welcome back to the exciting world of Feng Shui! In this section, we will delve deeper into enhancing the health and abundance in your kitchen. Get ready to transform this space into a hub of positive energy and prosperity!

The kitchen is not just any room in your house; it is the heart and soul of your home. It nourishes your body, mind, and spirit. By implementing Feng Shui principles in this sacred space, you can improve your well-being and attract abundance into your life. Let's dive into some valuable tips and remedies to create a harmonious and uplifting environment in your kitchen.

Color has a profound impact on our emotions and energy. By choosing the right colors for your kitchen, you can enhance its energy and promote health and abundance. The colors that resonate well with the Feng Shui principles are earthy tones such as warm yellows, soft greens, and rich browns. These colors represent nourishment, growth, and stability.

If your kitchen is already painted in vibrant or bold colors, don't worry! You can incorporate the appropriate tones through accessories and decor. Add some earthy elements like potted plants, wooden utensils, or earth-toned curtains. These simple touches will infuse positive energy and create a balanced atmosphere.

Clutter is like stagnant energy that hinders the flow of positive chi (energy) in your kitchen. It's time to get rid of unnecessary items, expired food, and broken appliances. A clutter-free kitchen allows for smooth energy circulation and promotes a sense of tranquility and organization.

Start by decluttering your countertops. Keep only the essential items that you use frequently. Store away appliances that are seldom used and keep your kitchen surfaces clean and tidy. Make use of storage solutions like cabinets, shelves, and drawers to maintain a clutter-free space. Remember, simplicity is key in creating an inviting and abundant kitchen.

The number three holds a special significance in Feng Shui. It symbolizes unity, harmony, and wholeness. You can harness this power by incorporating groupings of three in your kitchen. Place three matching items, such as vases, candles, or plants, on a countertop or shelf. This arrangement brings balance and positivity to the space and invites abundance into your life.

Don't limit yourself to just one set of three; you can create multiple groupings throughout your kitchen. Remember to choose items that resonate with you and make you feel joyful and abundant. Let the energy of three work its magic and watch your kitchen come alive with vitality and prosperity!

A truly balanced and abundant kitchen engages all the senses. Consider incorporating elements that appeal to each sense to create a harmonious environment. Here are some ideas to get you started:

- Visual appeal: Hang uplifting artwork or display fresh flowers to create a beautiful and inspiring space.
- Aromatherapy: Use essential oils or scented candles with invigorating scents like citrus or peppermint to stimulate your sense of smell.
- Pleasurable sounds: Play soothing music or the sounds of nature to create a serene ambiance while cooking or dining.
- Tactile sensations: Incorporate comfortable seating, soft fabrics, and textured materials to create a cozy and inviting atmosphere.
- Taste sensations: Fill your kitchen with nutritious and delicious foods that nourish your body and enhance your well-being.

Good lighting is vital in Feng Shui to promote positive energy flow. Proper illumination not only enhances the aesthetics of your kitchen but also influences your mood and well-being. Let natural light flood into your kitchen by keeping windows clean and unobstructed. If natural light is limited, opt for warm, soft lighting fixtures that create a welcoming and cozy atmosphere.

Additionally, consider adding task lighting for specific areas where you perform tasks like chopping vegetables or reading recipes. Adjustable lighting in these areas ensures you have the right amount of light for different activities, promoting efficiency and well-being.

I hope these Feng Shui tips and remedies will inspire you to create a space that nurtures your health and attracts abundance. Your kitchen is more than just a place to cook; it is a gateway to nourishment, well-being, and prosperity. Embrace the principles of Feng Shui in your kitchen, and watch the positive energy transform your life!

Chapter 9: Feng Shui for Wealth and Prosperity

Activating Wealth Areas in Your Home

Now that we have discovered the specific areas of your home that are associated with wealth and abundance in Feng Shui, it's time to learn how to activate and enhance the energy flow in these wealth areas.

In this subchapter, I will guide you through the process of activating the wealth areas in your home. By implementing these techniques, you can unlock the full potential of these areas and invite prosperity into your life.

The first step in activating your wealth areas is to declutter and clean them. Remove any unnecessary items and create a space that feels open and inviting. This will allow the energy, or chi, to flow freely and attract abundance.

Once you have decluttered, it's time to introduce elements that represent wealth and abundance. These elements can include symbols like wealth vases, money plants, or a wealth bowl filled with crystals. Place these items strategically in your wealth areas to amplify their energy.

In addition to symbols, you can also use colors to enhance the energy in your wealth areas. The colors associated with wealth in Feng Shui are purple, red, green, and gold. Consider incorporating these colors through artwork, cushions, or accessories in your wealth areas.

Another important aspect of activating your wealth areas is the use of lighting. Bright, natural light is ideal for these areas as it energizes the space. If natural light is limited, you can use artificial lighting such as lamps or spotlights to create a vibrant and illuminated environment.

To further enhance the energy in your wealth areas, consider adding mirrors. Mirrors are believed to multiply the energy in a space, so placing them strategically can help to attract and expand wealth. However, avoid placing mirrors directly facing the entrance of your wealth areas as this can cause the energy to bounce back out.

Lastly, it's important to consistently maintain and refresh the energy in your wealth areas. This can be done through regular cleaning, rearranging, and updating of the elements and symbols. By keeping these areas vibrant and alive, you are actively inviting abundance into your life.

So, are you ready to activate your wealth areas and invite prosperity into your home? Follow these techniques and watch as your abundance grows!

Attracting Prosperity with Feng Shui Cures

I am so excited to continue our journey into the fascinating world of Feng Shui remedies and symbols to attract wealth and prosperity. In this section, we will dive deeper into the specific cures and enhancements that can create a prosperous and abundant environment for you.

When it comes to attracting prosperity, Feng Shui offers a variety of remedies that can help you manifest your financial goals and create a thriving atmosphere. These remedies are based on principles that have been passed down through generations, and many people have experienced positive results by implementing them in their homes and workplaces.

One of the most popular Feng Shui cures for attracting wealth is the use of wealth symbols. These symbols, such as the Money Frog or the Wealth Vase, are believed to bring good fortune and abundance into your life. Placing these symbols in strategic locations, such as the southeast corner of your home or office, can help activate the energy of wealth and attract opportunities for financial growth.

Another powerful Feng Shui cure for prosperity is the use of mirrors. Mirrors are believed to double the energy and abundance in a space, so placing them strategically can amplify the positive vibrations of wealth. However, it's important to use them wisely and avoid placing them directly facing the main entrance or reflecting cluttered or negative areas, as this can hinder the flow of energy.

In addition to symbols and mirrors, Feng Shui also emphasizes the importance of maintaining a clutter-free and organized environment. Clutter is considered stagnant energy that can block the flow of wealth and abundance. By decluttering your space and creating a harmonious flow of energy, you can create a fertile ground for prosperity to enter your life.

Furthermore, incorporating the element of water into your space can also stimulate the flow of wealth. Consider adding a small indoor fountain or placing a fish tank with lively fish in the southeast corner of your home or office. Water represents abundance and prosperity in Feng Shui, and its presence can attract money and good fortune.

Lastly, it's important to have a positive mindset and believe in the power of Feng Shui. Your intentions and beliefs play a significant role in manifesting abundance, so approach the remedies and enhancements with a motivated and optimistic attitude. Trust that the universe will support your financial goals and that your efforts in implementing Feng Shui cures will yield positive results.

Remember, attracting prosperity with Feng Shui is a journey that requires dedication and consistent effort. By incorporating these remedies and enhancements into your life, you are taking an active role in creating a prosperous and abundant environment that can support your financial aspirations. So let's embark on this exciting journey together and manifest the wealth and prosperity you deserve!

Creating a Wealth-Attracting Altar

Now that you've learned the basics of Feng Shui, it's time to dive into the exciting world of creating a Feng Shui altar for manifesting wealth and abundance. Are you ready to activate the energy of wealth in your space? Let's get started!

Creating a Wealth-Attracting Altar is an essential step in harnessing the power of Feng Shui to enhance your financial prosperity. By carefully selecting the right elements and executing specific rituals, you can create a sacred space that vibrates with abundance.

First and foremost, let's talk about the location of your altar. In Feng Shui, the southeast corner of your home or office is associated with wealth and abundance. This is the ideal spot to set up your altar. Find a surface, such as a table or shelf, that can serve as the foundation for your altar.

Next, let's discuss the elements that can attract wealth energy to your altar. One popular element is a bowl of water, symbolizing the flow of abundance. You can also include objects that represent wealth, such as crystals, coins, or a green plant, which is believed to bring financial growth.

As you arrange these elements on your altar, be mindful of the principles of balance and harmony. Arrange them in a way that feels visually pleasing and energetically balanced. Remember, Feng Shui is all about creating a harmonious environment that supports your intentions.

Now that you have your altar set up, it's time to activate its energy. One powerful ritual you can perform is lighting a green candle while visualizing your financial goals. As the flame flickers and illuminates the space, imagine yourself already living a life of abundance. Feel the excitement and gratitude that comes with financial prosperity.

In addition to the candle ritual, you can also incorporate affirmations and mantras into your daily practice. Repeat positive statements about wealth and abundance, such as I am open to receiving unlimited financial blessings or Money flows to me easily and effortlessly. By affirming these statements regularly, you are aligning your mindset with the energy of abundance.

Remember, a Feng Shui altar is a sacred space for manifestation, so it's essential to keep it clean and clutter-free. Regularly dust the surfaces, remove any stagnant energy, and replenish the elements as needed.

Creating a Wealth-Attracting Altar is a powerful practice that can support you on your journey to financial prosperity. By infusing your intentions and energy into this sacred space, you are inviting the energy of abundance to flow into your life. Get creative, trust your intuition, and enjoy the process of crafting a Feng Shui altar that truly resonates with your desires.

Chapter 10: Feng Shui for Career Success

Optimizing Your Workspace with Feng Shui

Now that we've covered the basics of Feng Shui and how it can positively impact our workspaces, let's dive into the practical aspect of optimizing your workspace with Feng Shui. By making some intentional adjustments, you can create a space that not only promotes productivity but also inspires and motivates you to achieve career success.

The first step in optimizing your workspace is to declutter and organize. Clutter can create a stagnant and chaotic energy, hindering your focus and creativity. Take the time to go through your workspace and get rid of any unnecessary items. Keep only what you need and love, and find designated spaces for each item.

Next, let's talk about desk placement. According to Feng Shui principles, your desk should be placed in what's called the commanding position. This means that you should have a clear view of the room's entrance while sitting at your desk. This position allows you to feel more in control and aware of your surroundings, enhancing your sense of confidence and authority.

Now, let's focus on the elements in your workspace. Each element has its own energy and can help bring balance and harmony to your space. Here are some tips on how to incorporate the five elements of Feng Shui:

- **Wood:** Add plants or wooden furniture to bring in the energy of growth and vitality.
- **Fire:** Place a candle or a lamp in the Fame area (the back center of your desk) to ignite passion and inspiration.
- **Earth:** Use earthy colors or add a small potted plant to create a sense of stability and grounding.
- **Metal:** Incorporate metal objects such as a desk organizer or a metal frame to enhance clarity and focus.
- **Water:** Add a small tabletop fountain or a picture of a serene water scene to invite the energy of flow and abundance.

In addition to these elemental adjustments, it's important to pay attention to the lighting in your workspace. Natural light is ideal, so try to position your desk near a window to receive ample daylight. If natural light is limited, invest in a good desk lamp that mimics natural light to avoid harsh artificial lighting.

Lastly, let's discuss the power of personalization. Your workspace should reflect your personality and inspire you. Surround yourself with meaningful items such as vision boards, motivational quotes, or artwork that resonates with your goals and aspirations. By creating a space that speaks to you, you'll feel more connected and motivated to work towards your career success.

Remember, Feng Shui is not just about rearranging furniture or adding plants; it's about creating a space that supports and nourishes your energy. Take the time to apply these Feng Shui principles to your workspace, and you'll notice a positive shift in your focus, productivity, and overall career success.

Activating Career Areas for Success

In this subchapter, we will explore how to activate the career areas in your home or office to promote success and professional growth. By harnessing the power of Feng Shui, we can create an environment that energizes and supports our career aspirations.

Activating the career areas in your space is essential for inviting opportunities and advancement in your professional life. These specific areas have a direct impact on your career path and can greatly influence your success.

Let's dive into some practical tips for activating career areas and setting the stage for success:

1. Clear the clutter: Decluttering is the first step in any Feng Shui practice. Get rid of any unnecessary items or papers that are taking up space in your career areas. A clutter-free environment promotes clarity and focus, allowing for new opportunities to flow.

2. Enhance with the element of water: Water represents career growth and opportunities in Feng Shui. Introduce water elements such as a small fountain or a fish tank in the career areas of your space. The flowing water symbolizes progress and forward movement in your professional life.

3. Use plants for growth and vitality: Plants bring vibrant energy and life-force into any space. Place green plants or fresh flowers in your career

areas to promote growth and vitality. Choose plants with rounded or upward-growing leaves to symbolize upward career movement.

4. Incorporate the color black: The color black embodies the energy of depth, strength, and resilience. Introduce black accents such as throw pillows, artwork, or office accessories in your career areas to promote a sense of power and authority.

5. Add meaningful symbols: Symbols can have a significant impact on our subconscious mind and evoke positive feelings and emotions. Place objects or artwork that symbolize success, abundance, or your desired career outcomes in your career areas. These symbols will serve as constant reminders of your professional goals.

Remember, activating career areas is not a one-time task. It requires ongoing attention and intention. Regularly review and refresh your career areas to keep the energy flowing and evolving.

By implementing these Feng Shui practices, you can create a supportive environment that aligns with your career aspirations and fosters professional growth. Stay motivated, put in the effort, and watch as new opportunities and success come your way!

Boosting Professional Growth and Opportunities

Are you ready to take your professional development to the next level? In this subchapter, we will explore how implementing Feng Shui strategies can boost your professional growth and attract new opportunities. Let's dive in!

Feng Shui is the ancient art of arranging your surroundings to create harmony and balance. By applying Feng Shui principles to your workspace, you can enhance the flow of positive energy, or chi, and create an environment that supports your career goals. Let's explore some practical tips to get started.

1. Clear Clutter: Clutter can create mental and physical barriers, hindering your professional growth. Start by decluttering your workspace, eliminating any unnecessary items that are taking up space. Keep your desk clean and organized to promote productivity and focus.

2. Optimize Desk Placement: The placement of your desk can significantly impact your professional development. Position your desk in the command position, with a clear view of the room's entrance. This placement enhances your sense of control and allows you to be aware of new opportunities as they arise.

3. Use Colors Strategically: Colors have a profound effect on our emotions and energy levels. Incorporate colors that support your career goals into your workspace. For example, blue represents calmness and professionalism, while green symbolizes growth and abundance.

4. Enhance the Career Bagua Area: The Bagua is a Feng Shui energy map that divides your space into nine areas, each corresponding to a different aspect of your life. To boost professional growth, focus on enhancing the Career Bagua area. Add elements like a small plant or a meaningful piece of artwork that represents your career aspirations.

5. Increase Natural Light: Natural light has a positive impact on productivity and mood. If possible, position your desk near a window to maximize the amount of natural light in your workspace. If natural light is limited, consider using full-spectrum light bulbs that mimic natural sunlight.

6. Incorporate Inspirational Items: Surround yourself with items that inspire and motivate you. Whether it's a vision board displaying your career goals, inspirational quotes, or meaningful objects, having these reminders in your workspace can fuel your professional development.

7. Create a Welcoming Entrance: The entrance to your workspace sets the tone for your professional development. Make sure it is clutter-free and welcoming. Add elements like a doormat or a small plant to invite positive energy into your space.

8. Use Feng Shui Enhancements: Explore the use of Feng Shui enhancements such as mirrors, crystals, or wind chimes to further enhance the positive energy in your workspace. These items can help redirect and amplify chi, supporting your professional growth.

9. Simplify Your Technology: Technology is an essential part of our professional lives, but it can also create distractions and overwhelm. Simplify your technology by organizing your digital files, minimizing notifications, and creating a dedicated workspace for your devices.

10. Practice Mindfulness: Finally, remember to prioritize self-care and mindfulness in your professional development journey. Take regular breaks, practice deep breathing exercises, and set aside time for reflection and goal setting.

By implementing these Feng Shui strategies, you can create a workspace that supports your career goals and attracts new opportunities. Embrace the power of Feng Shui and watch as your professional growth soars!

Chapter 11: Feng Shui for Health and Well-being

Creating a Healing Sanctuary at Home

Welcome to the continuation of our journey into the world of Feng Shui! In the previous chapter, we explored the concept of the healing sanctuary and its importance for health and well-being. Now, we are going to delve deeper into the practical aspects of creating a nurturing and supportive environment for physical and emotional healing.

Creating a healing sanctuary at home is a wonderful way to cultivate a space that promotes serenity, rejuvenation, and balance. By incorporating the principles of Feng Shui, we can amplify the positive energy flow within our surroundings and enhance our overall well-being.

So, how can we begin transforming our living spaces into healing sanctuaries? Let's dive into some key elements and practices that can help us achieve this:

A cluttered space often leads to a cluttered mind. To create a healing sanctuary, it's essential to declutter and organize your home. Start by identifying areas that need attention and go through your belongings systematically. The goal is to create a clean and harmonious environment where energy can flow freely.

Set aside some time each week to tackle a specific area of your home. Sort through your belongings and ask yourself, Does this item bring me joy? Does it serve a practical purpose? If the answer is no, consider donating or discarding it. Embrace the concept of minimalism and let go of what no longer serves you.

Colors play a significant role in creating a healing sanctuary. In Feng Shui, each color represents different elements and energy. For a soothing and calming ambiance, opt for soft, earthy tones such as gentle blues, muted greens, and warm neutral shades.

Create an intentional color palette that resonates with you and promotes relaxation. Consider painting your walls in calming hues or incorporating these shades through furnishings, artwork, and décor items. Remember, the goal is to create a space where you feel nurtured and supported.

Nature has a profound impact on our well-being, so it's essential to incorporate natural elements into our healing sanctuaries. Introduce plants, fresh flowers, and natural materials such as wood, stone, and bamboo to create a connection with the outdoors.

Plants not only add a touch of greenery but also purify the air and promote a sense of tranquility. Place them strategically in areas where you spend the most time, such as your bedroom or living room. Surround yourself with natural materials that evoke a sense of grounding and calmness.

Lighting can greatly influence the energy flow within a space. Aim for a balance between natural and artificial lighting to create a soothing and harmonious atmosphere. Natural light is the ideal choice, as it is invigorating and promotes a sense of vitality.

If natural light is limited, incorporate gentle, warm-toned artificial lighting to mimic the sun's glow. Avoid harsh fluorescent lights and instead opt for softer, diffused lighting options. Use dimmers to adjust the lighting according to your mood and activity.

Designate a specific area in your home as a sacred space for meditation, reflection, or prayer. This can be a corner in your bedroom, a nook in your living room, or even a dedicated room if you have the space.

Personalize this space with items that hold deep meaning for you. It could be a beautiful altar with candles, crystals, or religious artifacts, or simply a comfortable meditation cushion and a peaceful painting. This sacred space will serve as a haven for you to retreat to whenever you need a moment of solace and rejuvenation.

By implementing these practices, you can create a healing sanctuary at home that supports your physical and emotional well-being.

Remember, the key is to infuse your space with intention, mindfulness, and a genuine desire to cultivate a nurturing environment. So go ahead and start transforming your home into a sanctuary of healing and renewal!

Harmonizing Health Areas with Feng Shui

When it comes to creating a harmonious and balanced home, Feng Shui offers valuable insights into the areas of our living spaces that can affect our health and well-being. By understanding the specific areas in our homes that are associated with health, we can take proactive steps to enhance the energy flow and promote positive vibes in those spaces. Let's dive deeper into these health areas and discover how we can make the most of Feng Shui principles to create a nurturing environment.

Now that we have a good understanding of the health areas in our homes, it's time to put the principles of Feng Shui into action. By employing specific techniques, we can create a harmonious balance and enhance the energy flow in these areas, leading to improved health and overall well-being. Let's explore some practical tips and tricks to harmonize our health areas with Feng Shui.

Harmonizing Health Areas with Feng Shui:

It's exciting to discover how Feng Shui can transform our living spaces into sanctuaries of health and wellness. By applying the following techniques, we can cultivate positive energy and create an environment that supports our well-being:

1. Clear the Clutter: Start by decluttering and organizing the health areas in your home. Removing excess items not only creates a sense of spaciousness but also allows energy to flow freely.

2. Introduce Natural Elements: Incorporate natural elements such as plants, crystals, and water features into your health areas. These elements not only add beauty but also promote a sense of tranquility and healing.

3. Color Therapy: Choose colors that correspond to the specific health areas you want to enhance. For example, green represents growth

and vitality, making it an ideal color for the health area in your home. Experiment with different hues to find what resonates with you.

4. Light it Up: Good lighting is essential for promoting a vibrant and healthy atmosphere. Ensure that your health areas receive ample natural light during the day and incorporate soft, ambient lighting for the evenings.

5. Balance the Five Elements: According to Feng Shui principles, the five elements (wood, fire, earth, metal, and water) should be in harmony within your health areas. Introduce items or colors representing each element to create a balanced energy flow.

Remember, Feng Shui is not just about arranging furniture or decorating our living spaces - it's about creating an environment that supports our health and well-being on a deeper level. By applying these techniques, we can align with the positive energy of our health areas and experience the benefits that come with it.

Enhancing Physical and Emotional Well-being

In this section, we will explore practical tips and remedies to enhance your physical and emotional well-being using Feng Shui. By understanding the principles of this ancient practice, you can create a harmonious and balanced environment that supports your overall health and happiness.

Feng Shui is not just about arranging furniture and decorations; it is a holistic approach that takes into account the flow of energy, or qi, in your space. By harmonizing the energy in your surroundings, you can positively impact different aspects of your life, including your physical and emotional well-being.

Now, let's dive into some specific ways in which you can enhance your well-being through Feng Shui:

1. Clearing Clutter: One of the foundational principles of Feng Shui is keeping your space free of clutter. When your surroundings are cluttered, the energy becomes stagnant, hindering the flow of positive energy. By decluttering and organizing your environment, you create a sense of calm and invite positive energy into your space. Take the time to go through your belongings and let go of items that no longer serve you.

2. Creating a Balanced Layout: Another aspect of Feng Shui is the arrangement of furniture and objects in a room. Aim for a balanced layout that allows for the smooth flow of energy. Avoid placing furniture in a way that obstructs pathways or creates a sense of imbalance. Optimize the positioning of your furniture to create a harmonious and inviting atmosphere.

3. Incorporating Nature: Connecting with nature is essential for our well-being. In Feng Shui, incorporating elements of nature, such as plants and natural materials, can help create a sense of grounding and balance. Introduce indoor plants into your space to purify the air and bring a touch of nature indoors. Use natural materials, such as wood and stone, in your decor to add warmth and tranquility.

4. Balancing the Five Elements: The five elements - wood, fire, earth, metal, and water - play a significant role in Feng Shui. Each element represents different aspects of life and can be harnessed to create balance. Evaluate the presence of these elements in your space and make adjustments if necessary. For example, if your space lacks the element of water, you can incorporate a small fountain or a representation of water to restore balance.

5. Optimizing the Bedroom: Your bedroom is a crucial space for your physical and emotional well-being. Ensure that it is a calming and restful environment. Position your bed in a way that provides a clear view of the door without being directly in line with it. Use soothing colors and soft lighting to create a serene atmosphere. Remove any electronics or distractions that may interfere with a good night's sleep.

By implementing these practical tips and remedies, you can begin to enhance your physical and emotional well-being through the principles of Feng Shui. Remember, the key is to create a harmonious and balanced environment that supports your overall health and happiness.

Chapter 12: Feng Shui for Love and Relationships

Balancing Relational Energies in Your Home

Creating a harmonious and supportive environment for healthy relationships is crucial for maintaining balance and harmony in our lives. When we are surrounded by positive energy, it can greatly enhance our relationships and overall well-being.

One key aspect of achieving energetic balance is understanding the interplay between our surroundings and our internal energy. Our homes hold a special significance in shaping our relationships, as they act as a sanctuary for our love and connection. By harnessing the power of Feng Shui, we can optimize our living spaces to create an environment that supports and fosters healthy relationships.

Feng Shui, an ancient Chinese practice, focuses on the arrangement and positioning of objects in our surroundings to promote positive energy flow. By following simple Feng Shui techniques, we can create a space that encourages love, unity, and happiness.

Balancing Relational Energies in Your Home:

Now, let's delve into some practical tips and techniques to balance the relational energies in your home. Implementing these strategies can have a profound impact on your relationships and help you cultivate a harmonious and loving atmosphere:

1. **Clear the Clutter:** Clutter in our living spaces has a direct impact on our energy levels and can disrupt the flow of positive energy. Start by decluttering your home and letting go of any unnecessary belongings. This will create a clean and open space for love and positive energies to thrive.
2. **Enhance the Relationship Corner:** According to Feng Shui principles, the relationship corner of your home is located in

the far right corner from the entrance. Pay special attention to this area and decorate it with symbols of love and connection, such as artwork, candles, or fresh flowers. This will help to enhance the energy of love and harmony in your relationships.

3. **Balance Yin and Yang:** In Feng Shui, the concept of yin and yang represents the balance between two opposing energies. Create a balanced environment by incorporating both yin and yang elements. For example, you can combine soft, flowing curtains (yin) with bold, vibrant colors (yang) to create a harmonious atmosphere that promotes love and balance.

4. **Utilize the Five Elements:** The five elements of Feng Shui - Wood, Fire, Earth, Metal, and Water - play a vital role in creating a balanced and harmonious space. Incorporate these elements strategically into your home through colors, textures, and materials. For instance, you can use plants or wooden furniture to bring in the Wood element or add a water feature to enhance the Water element. This will create a harmonizing effect on your relationships.

5. **Ensure Good Air Quality:** The quality of air in our homes directly impacts our physical and emotional well-being. Make sure to open windows regularly to allow fresh air to circulate and consider using air-purifying plants to improve the air quality. By ensuring good air quality, you are promoting a healthy environment for love and relationships to flourish.

By implementing these simple yet powerful Feng Shui techniques, you can create a space that not only supports healthy relationships but also fosters a sense of love and harmony in all aspects of your life.

Attracting and Nurturing Romantic Relationships

In this subchapter, we will explore the fascinating world of Feng Shui practices that can help you attract and nurture romantic relationships.

Whether you are single and seeking love or already in a relationship and looking to deepen the connection, Feng Shui can be an incredible tool to enhance the energy of love and romance in your life.

Let's dive in and discover some powerful techniques for attracting and nurturing romantic relationships with Feng Shui:

The Love Corner, also known as the Relationship Corner, is a key area in your home or room that directly influences your love life. By clearing this space of clutter and activating it with symbols of love, you can create a magnetizing energy that attracts romance into your life. I will guide you on how to find and enhance your Love Corner for maximum effect.

Creating a balance between yin and yang energy is essential for a harmonious and loving relationship. I will show you how to identify areas in your home where the energy may be imbalanced and provide tips on how to restore harmony. By promoting a balanced energy flow, you can create an environment that supports and nurtures love.

The colors and lighting in your space can greatly impact the atmosphere and set the mood for romance. I will share with you which colors and lighting techniques are most beneficial for creating a romantic ambiance. By harnessing the power of color and lighting, you can create an environment that evokes love and intimacy.

Each element in Feng Shui represents different aspects of life, including love and relationships. By incorporating specific elements into your space, you can enhance the energy of love and promote harmony in your relationships. I will provide guidance on how to incorporate these elements in a way that aligns with your personal preferences and style.

The bedroom is a sacred space where intimacy and connection thrive. I will share practical tips and suggestions on how to create a nurturing and sensual environment in your bedroom. From arranging furniture to choosing the right bedding, you will learn how to transform your bedroom into a haven of love and pleasure.

In order to attract and nurture a healthy relationship, it is important to first cultivate self-love and self-care. I will guide you on how to create a self-care routine and establish practices that nourish and uplift your spirit. By prioritizing self-love, you will radiate a positive energy that naturally attracts love and fulfillment into your life.

These are just a few of the powerful techniques that you will explore in this subchapter. By incorporating the principles of Feng Shui into your life, you can create an environment that supports and enhances love and romance. Get ready to embark on a transformative journey as we delve into the world of Feng Shui for attracting and nurturing romantic relationships!

Strengthening Family and Social Connections

Now that we've explored the principles of Feng Shui and how they can enhance our family relationships and social connections, let's delve deeper into some practical strategies to strengthen these bonds.

Family is the foundation of our lives, and nurturing strong relationships within our family unit is crucial for a harmonious and fulfilling life. By applying Feng Shui principles through simple changes in our environment, we can create a space that supports love, understanding, and growth.

One effective way to strengthen family connections is by creating a designated area for quality time and bonding. This can be a cozy corner in the living room or a dedicated space where family photos, keepsakes, and memories are displayed. By giving importance to these items, we reinforce the sense of belonging and love within the family. In Feng Shui, this area is known as the Family or Relationship corner, and it can be enhanced by incorporating elements like soft lighting, comfortable seating, and vibrant colors.

Another aspect to consider is the layout of our living space. Feng Shui encourages an open and flowing design that allows energy, or chi, to move freely. This can be achieved by removing any clutter or obstacles that hinder the energy flow and by arranging furniture in a way that promotes communication and interaction. For example, positioning sofas and chairs in a circular or semicircular arrangement encourages face-to-face conversations and creates a welcoming atmosphere.

Creating a harmonious environment that supports strong bonds and positive interactions extends beyond our immediate family. It encompasses our social connections as well. To enhance these relationships, we can focus on the Friendship or Helpful People corner of our living space. Adding meaningful artwork, symbols, or objects related to friendship or collaboration can attract positive energy and contribute to the development of a supportive social network.

In addition to physical changes in our environment, it is also essential to cultivate an attitude of open-mindedness, empathy, and kindness. Feng Shui teaches us that our thoughts and intentions affect the energy around us. By consciously fostering positive thoughts and expressing gratitude, we create an energetic field that draws people towards us and strengthens our social connections.

Remember, incorporating Feng Shui principles into our lives is an ongoing process and may require some experimentation. As you explore and implement these strategies, observe the changes in your family and social dynamics. Embrace the journey of self-discovery and watch as the positive energy flows into every aspect of your life.

Chapter 13: Feng Shui for Children's Spaces

Creating a Nurturing Environment for Children

Creating a nurturing environment for children is essential for their overall well-being and development. As a parent or caregiver, you have the power to create a space that fosters positive energy and supports their growth. In this section, I will share some Feng Shui tips and ideas to help you design a child-friendly space that promotes a sense of harmony and positivity.

First and foremost, it's important to declutter your child's room. A cluttered space can lead to scattered energy and hinder their ability to concentrate and relax. Encourage your child to keep their belongings organized and create designated storage areas for toys, books, and clothes. This not only promotes cleanliness but also allows energy to flow freely throughout the room.

Next, consider the placement of furniture in the room. According to Feng Shui principles, it's best to position the bed against a solid wall, ensuring a sense of stability and security for your child. Avoid placing the bed directly in line with the door, as this can create a sense of unease and restlessness. Instead, position it diagonally across from the door to provide a sense of balance and harmony.

Furthermore, incorporating elements of nature can have a calming effect on your child's space. Consider adding plants or a small indoor herb garden to introduce nature into their environment. Not only do plants improve air quality, but they also create a sense of serenity and connection with the natural world.

Lighting is another important aspect to consider in a child's room. Opt for natural light whenever possible, as it has a positive effect on mood and overall well-being. If natural light is limited, choose soft and warm artificial lighting options to create a cozy and inviting atmosphere.

Lastly, personalization is key in creating a nurturing space for your child. Allow them to have a say in the design and decoration of their room. Incorporate elements that reflect their interests, hobbies, and personality. This not only promotes a sense of ownership but also allows them to feel comfortable and supported in their own space.

Feng Shui Tips for Children's Bedrooms

Now that we have learned the basics of Feng Shui and its principles, let's dive into some specific tips for creating harmonious and stimulating bedrooms for children. By implementing these design and decor strategies, we can promote learning, creativity, and restful sleep.

1. Clear the Clutter:

One of the fundamental principles of Feng Shui is to create a clutter-free environment. This applies to children's bedrooms as well. Encourage your child to keep their room tidy by providing them with ample storage solutions, such as bins, shelves, and drawers. This will not only promote a sense of order but also allow positive energy to flow freely.

2. Balanced Placement of Furniture:

Arrange the furniture in a way that creates a sense of balance and harmony. Avoid placing the bed directly in line with the door, as this can create an unsettling energy. Instead, position the bed diagonally from the door or against a solid wall to create a sense of security and stability for your child.

3. Use Soothing Colors:

The choice of colors in a child's bedroom can have a significant impact on their mood and well-being. Opt for soothing colors like pastels or light shades of blue, green, or pink. These colors promote relaxation and a peaceful atmosphere, enabling your child to rest and recharge.

4. Incorporate Natural Elements:

Bringing nature indoors can enhance the positive energy in a child's bedroom. Use natural materials such as wood, cotton, and plants. Adding a small indoor plant or a nature-inspired artwork can create a sense of connection to the outdoors, which can have a calming effect on your child's mind.

5. Create a Study Area:

Designate a specific area in the bedroom for your child's study or creative endeavors. This area should be well-lit and free from distractions. Use proper desk and chair ergonomics to support good posture and concentration. Consider placing a vision board or inspirational quotes to motivate and inspire your child.

6. Symbolism and Personalization:

Add meaningful symbols or decorations in your child's bedroom to create a personal and nurturing space. This could be a charm or a favorite toy that holds a special meaning to your child. Personalization helps create a sense of ownership and comfort, making the bedroom a place of expression and positive energy.

Remember, these tips are just the beginning. As you explore and apply Feng Shui principles to your child's bedroom, observe how they respond to the changes. Every child is unique, and their needs may vary. Adjust and experiment to find what works best for them, creating a space that fosters their growth, creativity, and peaceful sleep.

Enhancing Learning and Creativity in Kids' Spaces

Now that we have explored the fascinating world of Feng Shui techniques to stimulate learning and creativity in children's spaces, let us dive deeper into creating an environment that supports your child's intellectual and artistic development. This subchapter will provide you with practical tips and insights on enhancing learning and creativity in kids' spaces. Let's get started!

When it comes to fostering a love for learning and creativity in our children, the environment plays a crucial role. By creating a stimulating environment, we can inspire and motivate our kids to explore their interests and express themselves freely. Here are some key tips:

- Incorporate vibrant colors: Colors have a profound impact on our mood and energy levels. Opt for bright and lively colors like red, orange, and yellow to promote enthusiasm and creativity in your child's space.
- Organize and declutter: A clutter-free environment promotes clarity of thought and enhances productivity. Encourage your child to regularly declutter their space and keep it organized. Provide ample storage solutions to keep their belongings neatly arranged.
- Introduce natural elements: Connecting with nature has a calming effect on our minds. Bring elements of nature into your child's space, such as plants, natural light, and materials like wood, to create a harmonious and tranquil atmosphere.
- Personalize the space: Let your child be involved in the process of decorating their room. Encourage them to express their personality and interests through artwork, posters, and personal mementos. This will give them a sense of ownership and pride in their space.

The layout of your child's space can significantly impact their learning and creativity. A well-thought-out design can enhance focus, productivity, and imagination. Here are some design tips to consider:

- Create defined zones: Divide the space into different zones based on specific activities like studying, reading, and playing. This will help your child mentally switch gears and stay focused on the task at hand.
- Ensure proper lighting: Good lighting is essential for concentration and visual comfort. Provide a mix of natural and artificial lighting, and ensure that the workspace has adequate

task lighting to minimize eye strain.

- Optimize furniture placement: Arrange furniture in a way that promotes flow and easy movement. Make sure the desk or workspace is positioned to face a wall or window, avoiding distractions from behind.
- Incorporate ergonomic elements: A comfortable and supportive chair, as well as an adjustable desk height, are vital for maintaining good posture and preventing physical strain during long study sessions.

Encouraging creativity is essential for your child's overall development. By incorporating art and inspiration into their space, you can nurture their creative spirit. Here are some ideas to inspire and engage your child's imagination:

- Display their artwork: Showcase your child's artwork prominently in their room. This will not only boost their confidence but also serve as a visual reminder of their artistic abilities.
- Create a vision board: Help your child create a vision board filled with images and quotes that inspire them. This can serve as a powerful tool to set goals, visualize their dreams, and ignite their creativity.
- Provide artistic materials: Stock their space with a variety of art supplies like colored pencils, paints, and sketchbooks. Encourage them to explore different art forms and express themselves freely through creativity.
- Incorporate inspirational quotes: Inspire your child with motivational quotes and affirmations. Display them on the walls or incorporate them into decorative elements to create a positive and empowering atmosphere.

In addition to creating a conducive environment, it is important to cultivate a learning mindset in your child. By instilling certain habits and values, you can empower them to become lifelong learners. Here's how you can encourage a growth mindset in your child:

- Emphasize the value of effort: Teach your child that effort and perseverance are more important than innate talent. Encourage them to embrace challenges and view mistakes as opportunities for growth.
- Provide positive reinforcement: Acknowledge and praise your child's progress and achievements. Celebrate their small wins and encourage them to set achievable goals.
- Foster curiosity and exploration: Encourage your child to ask questions, explore new ideas, and seek answers. Support their curiosity by providing age-appropriate books, educational toys, and engaging activities.
- Promote a love for learning: Be a role model by showing enthusiasm for learning and sharing your own knowledge and experiences. Encourage regular reading, engage in intellectual discussions, and foster a love for knowledge.

Chapter 14: Feng Shui for Gardens and Outdoor Spaces

Harmonizing Outdoor Energies in Your Garden

Welcome back! In the previous chapter, we discussed the importance of energy flow and balance in your outdoor spaces. Now, let's dive deeper into the world of Feng Shui and explore how we can harmonize the energies in your garden to create a truly inviting and tranquil environment.

When it comes to Feng Shui, the principles can be applied not only to your home but also to your outdoor spaces. Your garden is a place where nature and energy come together, and by creating a harmonious balance, you can enhance the positive chi or energy that flows through it.

So, how do we go about harmonizing the energies in your garden? Let's start by understanding the concept of energy pathways or qi flow. This is the life force energy that circulates around your garden, and it's important to ensure that it flows smoothly and gracefully through the space.

One way to enhance the qi flow in your garden is by incorporating winding paths and curved walkways. These gentle curves help to slow down the energy and create a sense of harmony and tranquility. You can also use plants and shrubs to guide the energy along specific paths, creating a natural flow throughout the garden.

Another key aspect of harmonizing the energies in your garden is through the use of color. In Feng Shui, each color is associated with specific elements and has its own unique energy. By incorporating a variety of colors in your garden, you can create a balanced and vibrant space. For example, red is associated with fire and passion, while green represents growth and renewal. By using a combination of these colors, you can create a harmonious balance of energy in your outdoor space.

In addition to colors, the placement of objects in your garden also plays a vital role in harmonizing the energies. For example, placing a water feature, such as a fountain or pond, in the north or east area of your garden can enhance the flow of abundance and prosperity. Similarly, strategic placement of natural stones or sculptures can create a sense of grounding and stability.

One important tip to remember is to always keep your garden well-maintained and clutter-free. Clutter not only blocks the flow of energy but also creates a sense of chaos and imbalance. Regularly prune and trim your plants, clear away any debris, and create a sense of order in your outdoor space.

As you work on harmonizing the energies in your garden, remember that it's not just about creating a visually pleasing space but also about creating a space that nourishes your mind, body, and spirit. Take the time to connect with nature, meditate, and find moments of peace and serenity in your garden.

So, let's get started on harmonizing the energies in your garden and creating a truly harmonious and inviting space that will uplift and inspire you every day. Embrace the principles of Feng Shui and let the energy flow!

Creating Tranquil and Inviting Outdoor Retreats

Now that you have learned the basics of Feng Shui and its principles for creating a serene and peaceful environment, let's dive deeper into the topic and explore how to create tranquil and inviting outdoor retreats using these techniques. In this chapter, we will discuss various strategies and ideas that will help you design and arrange your outdoor spaces for relaxation and rejuvenation.

1. Choose the Right Elements for Your Outdoor Space

When designing your outdoor retreat, it's essential to select the right elements that align with the principles of Feng Shui. Consider incorporating natural materials like wood, stone, or bamboo to create a harmonious and balanced environment. These materials not only add an organic touch to your outdoor space but also symbolize stability and grounding.

2. Create Zones for Different Activities

Divide your outdoor space into different zones to accommodate various activities. This will help create a sense of organization and purpose in your retreat. Designate an area for relaxation where you can place comfortable seating, such as lounge chairs or hammocks. Create a separate space for dining and entertaining, where you can set up a cozy outdoor dining set or a fire pit for gatherings.

3. Incorporate Water Features

Water features, such as fountains, ponds, or waterfalls, have a calming effect on the mind and help create a serene atmosphere. Including a water element in your outdoor retreat can enhance the flow of energy and promote relaxation. Place a small fountain or a pond in a strategic location, ensuring that the water flows towards the center of your outdoor space, symbolizing the accumulation of positive energy.

4. Use Plants and Flowers to Bring Life

The presence of plants and flowers in your outdoor retreat can instantly uplift the mood and create a vibrant atmosphere. Choose a variety of plants that are known for their calming properties, such as lavender or jasmine. Incorporate plants with different textures, colors, and heights to add visual interest to your space. Don't forget to maintain them regularly to ensure they thrive and bring life to your retreat.

5. Create a Path to Relaxation

Design a pathway that leads you to your outdoor retreat, symbolizing a journey towards relaxation and tranquility. Use stepping stones or decorative tiles to create an inviting pathway. Consider planting fragrant herbs and flowers alongside the path to stimulate the senses further. Ensure that the pathway is well-lit during the evening to create a safe and enchanting ambiance.

6. Integrate Natural Lighting

Embrace natural lighting in your outdoor space as much as possible. The soft glow of the sun during the day creates a warm and welcoming atmosphere. Consider using outdoor curtains or blinds to filter the sunlight and create a gentle play of light and shadow. During the evening, incorporate soft and warm lighting elements, such as string lights or lanterns, to create an enchanting ambiance.

By implementing these strategies and ideas, you can transform your outdoor space into a tranquil and inviting retreat, where you can unwind, connect with nature, and find inner peace.

Remember, the key to creating a serene and peaceful outdoor environment lies in aligning with the principles of Feng Shui and using elements that promote relaxation and rejuvenation. Now, let's move on to the next chapter, where we will explore advanced techniques for enhancing your outdoor experience using Feng Shui.

Feng Shui Elements for Outdoor Balance

In the previous chapter, we explored the fascinating world of Feng Shui and how it can bring balance and harmony to our indoor spaces. Now, let's take this concept outdoors and discover how the five elements of Feng Shui can be applied in our gardens or outdoor areas. Nature has a powerful influence on our well-being, and incorporating Feng Shui principles in our outdoor spaces can enhance our connection with the natural world and create a harmonious environment.

The five elements of Feng Shui - Wood, Fire, Earth, Metal, and Water - are the fundamental building blocks of the universe. Each element has its own unique qualities and energies that can be harnessed to create balance and harmony in our surroundings. Let's delve deeper into how each element can be utilized in our outdoor spaces.

Wood: Representing growth and vitality, the Wood element can be introduced through the use of plants, trees, and wooden structures. By incorporating lush greenery and natural materials, we can create a sense of rejuvenation and vitality in our outdoor spaces. Consider planting trees that provide shade and a sense of grounding, and add wooden furniture or structures that blend seamlessly with the natural surroundings.

Fire: Fire symbolizes passion, transformation, and energy. To bring the Fire element into your garden, you can incorporate elements such as outdoor fire pits, candles, or even vibrant red and orange flowers. These elements will add warmth and create a focal point in your outdoor space, encouraging vitality and social interaction.

Earth: Grounding and stability are the essence of the Earth element. To enhance this element in your garden, consider using natural materials like stones, rocks, or clay pots. Create a sense of balance by incorporating earthy colors and textures throughout your outdoor space. You can also introduce the Earth element by planting low-maintenance, grounding plants that bring a sense of stability and tranquility.

Metal: Representing clarity and precision, the Metal element can be introduced through the use of metal sculptures, wind chimes, or even metallic-colored furniture. These elements will add a sense of elegance and refinement to your outdoor space. Incorporate metal accents strategically to create a harmonious balance between the other elements.

Water: The Water element symbolizes flow, calmness, and abundance. Introduce this element in your garden by incorporating features such as a pond, fountain, or even a birdbath. The sound and movement of water will create a soothing and serene atmosphere in your outdoor space. You can also incorporate blue or black colors to represent the Water element.

By understanding and utilizing the five elements of Feng Shui in your outdoor space, you can create a harmonious and balanced environment that promotes well-being and nourishes the soul. Embrace the beauty of nature and let the elements guide you in designing an outdoor space that brings you joy, peace, and a deeper connection with the world around you.

Chapter 15: Feng Shui for Personal Success and Growth

Cultivating Personal Development with Feng Shui

As we continue our exploration of Feng Shui and its impact on personal growth and development, let's now dive into the practical applications of this ancient practice. In this chapter, we will delve into how you can cultivate personal development through the power of Feng Shui.

When it comes to personal growth, our environment plays a crucial role in supporting and enhancing our journey. Feng Shui offers valuable insights and techniques to align our surroundings with our goals and aspirations. By harnessing the energy flow within our spaces, we can create a harmonious and supportive environment that nurtures our personal development. Let's explore some key ways in which Feng Shui can assist us in this endeavor.

The first step in cultivating personal development through Feng Shui is to create a balanced and harmonious space. A cluttered and disorganized environment can drain our energy and hinder our progress. By decluttering and organizing our surroundings, we can create a clear and peaceful atmosphere that promotes focus and clarity.

Consider the layout of your space and ensure that it allows for smooth energy flow. Arrange furniture and objects in a way that encourages movement and avoids blocking pathways. A well-structured space promotes a sense of calm and relaxation, providing a solid foundation for personal growth.

The Bagua Map is a powerful tool in Feng Shui that helps us identify and activate the different areas of our lives. By overlaying the Bagua Map onto our living space, we can connect specific areas with corresponding aspects of our lives, such as career, relationships, and health.

Take some time to analyze your space and identify which areas correspond to the important aspects of your personal development. Once you have determined the relevant sections, you can enhance them by incorporating specific Feng Shui remedies and enhancements. For example, you might introduce elements such as water features for career growth or symbols of love and partnership for enhancing relationships.

Colors, elements, and symbols play a significant role in Feng Shui. Each of these has unique properties and associations that can influence our energy and mindset. By consciously incorporating the right colors, elements, and symbols into our environment, we can create a conducive atmosphere for personal growth.

Consider the areas of your life that you wish to focus on and choose colors that correspond to those intentions. For example, if you are seeking greater creativity, you might incorporate shades of purple or orange in your workspace. Similarly, you can introduce elements such as plants, water, or earthy tones to foster specific qualities and energies.

Furthermore, symbols can serve as powerful reminders and anchors for our goals and aspirations. Displaying symbols, such as vision boards, affirmations, or meaningful artwork, can inspire and motivate us on our personal development journey.

In Feng Shui, cures and adjustments are used to rectify imbalances and enhance the flow of energy in our spaces. These can range from simple adjustments, such as rearranging furniture or adding mirrors to reflect light, to more complex remedies, such as incorporating specific objects or Feng Shui elements.

As you progress in your personal development, pay attention to any areas in your environment that may need adjustments or cures. This might involve identifying and addressing energy drains, creating a dedicated space for self-reflection and meditation, or introducing Feng Shui remedies specific to your intentions and goals.

Remember, Feng Shui is a journey, and its true power lies in the intention and mindfulness we bring to our surroundings. By aligning our environment with our personal growth and development, we can create a supportive and empowering space that propels us forward on our path.

Now that we have explored the ways in which Feng Shui can cultivate personal development, it's time to put these insights into action. In the next chapter, we will delve into practical techniques and exercises to help you align your environment with your goals and aspirations. Get ready to unleash the full potential of Feng Shui in manifesting your dreams and aspirations!

Enhancing Personal Achievement Areas

Now that you have discovered the specific areas of your home that are associated with personal achievement in Feng Shui, it's time to learn how to activate and optimize these areas to support your success and fulfillment.

In this subchapter, we will dive deeper into enhancing the personal achievement areas in your home. By making a few adjustments and incorporating some Feng Shui principles, you can create a space that energizes and inspires you to reach your goals.

Firstly, it's important to understand that enhancing the personal achievement areas is not just about physical changes to the space, but also about creating a positive and supportive mindset. While the physical changes help to align the energy in your home, your mindset plays a crucial role in attracting success and fulfillment.

One of the first things you can do to enhance these areas is to declutter and remove any items that are blocking the flow of energy. Clutter can create stagnant energy and hinder your progress. By clearing out the clutter, you create space for new opportunities and positive energy to flow.

In addition to decluttering, consider adding elements that symbolize success and achievement. For example, you could add a vision board or a display of your accomplishments in these areas. These visual reminders will help to keep you motivated and focused on your goals.

Another way to enhance the personal achievement areas is to incorporate the five elements of Feng Shui - wood, fire, earth, metal, and water. Each element carries its own energy and can be represented through colors, shapes, and materials. By including a balance of these elements in your decor, you create a harmonious and supportive environment for success.

Additionally, pay attention to the lighting in these areas. Good lighting helps to energize the space and improve your mood and productivity. Consider using natural light whenever possible or incorporating different lighting fixtures to create a warm and inviting atmosphere.

Lastly, remember to infuse these areas with your personal energy and intentions. Spend time in these spaces regularly, whether it's for work, studying, or pursuing your passions. The more you engage with these areas and align your actions with your goals, the more powerful the energy becomes.

As you work on enhancing the personal achievement areas in your home, remember that the changes you make should reflect your personal style and preferences. Feng Shui is a tool to help you create a supportive and nurturing environment, but it's essential to make it your own.

Now that you know how to enhance the personal achievement areas in your home, it's time to put these principles into action. Start making small adjustments and observe the positive impact it has on your mindset and success.

Stay motivated and keep working towards your goals. Success and fulfillment are within your reach!

Creating Positive Energy for Personal Growth

As we continue our journey into exploring the practices of Feng Shui, we dive deeper into the realm of creating positive energy for personal growth. Your quest for personal development and achieving your dreams begins here!

Creating a supportive and inspiring environment is crucial when it comes to cultivating positive energy. By harnessing the principles of Feng Shui, we can transform our spaces into nurturing sanctuaries that empower us to reach our full potential.

One of the fundamental aspects of Feng Shui is to declutter and organize your space. I know it may sound daunting at first, but trust me, the benefits are worth it! Start by tidying up one area at a time and let go of any items that no longer serve a purpose or bring you joy. It's amazing how much lighter you'll feel once you free yourself from the weight of unnecessary belongings.

Next, let's focus on the placement of furniture and objects in your space. When arranging your furniture, aim for openness and flow. Avoid blocking doorways or pathways, as this can hinder the natural energy, or chi, from circulating freely. Embrace natural light and fresh air by positioning your furniture to take advantage of these elements.

Colors play a significant role in Feng Shui as well. Incorporating calming and soothing hues, such as blues and greens, can promote a sense of tranquility. On the other hand, vibrant and energizing colors like red and orange can stimulate creativity and passion. Experiment with different color schemes to create the desired atmosphere for your personal growth journey.

Another essential aspect of Feng Shui is the use of plants and natural elements. Surrounding yourself with living greens not only adds aesthetic appeal but also purifies the air and promotes a sense of vitality. Explore options like succulents, peace lilies, or bamboo plants to enhance the positive energy in your space.

Lastly, don't underestimate the power of personal touches. Displaying meaningful artwork, photographs, or objects that inspire you can have a profound impact on your mindset. These cherished possessions remind you of your goals, aspirations, and the journey you are on. Let them serve as constant reminders of what you're working towards and the positive energy you are cultivating.

Remember, creating a supportive and inspiring environment is just the beginning. As you continue on your personal growth journey, be open to exploring and adjusting your space to align with your evolving goals and aspirations. Your environment has the power to shape your mindset, so take charge and create a space that fuels your dreams!

Don't miss out!

Visit the website below and you can sign up to receive emails whenever Margot Read publishes a new book. There's no charge and no obligation.

https://books2read.com/r/B-A-YIYDB-WXCXC

BOOKS 2 READ

Connecting independent readers to independent writers.

www.ingramcontent.com/pod-product-compliance
Lightning Source LLC
Chambersburg PA
CBHW051246160726
47994CB00003B/1047